W9-AOJ-162

WITHDRAWN

THE
SCARY HALLOWEEN
COSTUME BOOK

THE SCARY HALLOWEEN COSTUME BOOK

by Carol Barkin
and Elizabeth James

illustrated by Katherine Coville

Lothrop, Lee & Shepard Books
New York

For Bob, Tom, Susan,
Mike, and Nancy—
BOO!

Library of Congress Cataloging in Publication Data

Barkin, Carol.   The scary Halloween costume book.

Includes index.
Summary: Instructions for making a variety of easy and scary
outfits and creating ghoulish faces for Halloween.   1. Costume—
Juvenile literature.   2. Halloween—Juvenile literature.
[1. costume.   2. Halloween]   I. James, Elizabeth.   II. Coville,
Katherine, ill.   III. Title.   IV. Title: Halloween costume book.
TT633.B37   646'.47   81-14249
ISBN 0-688-00956-5   AACR2
ISBN 0-688-00957-3 (lib. bdg.)

CONTENTS

Safety Tips for Trick-or-Treating

GO AT A SAFE TIME
- Go trick-or-treating while it's still light outside.
- If you do go after dark, put reflective tape on your costume and your trick-or-treat bag. Carry a flashlight for extra visibility.

GO WITH SAFE PEOPLE
- Ask a parent or older brother or sister to go with you.
- If someone older isn't available, go with a *group* of your friends.
- *Never go trick-or-treating alone!*

WEAR A SAFE COSTUME
- Make sure you are able to move easily in your disguise.
- Make sure nothing blocks your eyes.
- Make sure you are *very visible* to passing drivers. (Again, reflective tape on your costume and bag will help you stand out.)

GO SAFE PLACES
- Plan your route ahead of time and *tell your parents where you'll be.*
- Pick well-lighted streets.
- If there are no sidewalks on your route, walk on the *left* side of the street, *facing traffic.*
- Cross only at corners. Never cross the street between parked cars or in the middle of the block.
- Wait until you get home to sort, check, and eat your treats.

TRICK OR TREAT!

Halloween is the one night of the year when you love to be scared and to scare everyone you meet. The fun of Halloween lies in thinking up the most terrifying disguise you can imagine and hearing everyone's gasps of fear, while at the same time you all know it's only make-believe.

No masks are needed to put together the scariest outfit in town. The costumes in this book are all quick, cheap, and easy to make. Best of all, you won't meet your double on every street corner. Putting together or making your own costume lets you use your own imagination to create a wonderfully horrifying look.

Read through the directions for the costume you plan to make to be sure you have all the elements needed. Most of the costume pieces are probably things you already have or can borrow or scrounge. If you do need to buy a piece of fabric or a pair of weird socks, shop

7

at the cheapest place you can find. After all, your outfit only has to last for one evening. It's going to be held together with staples or tape or safety pins—there's no sewing involved!

Be creative. If you don't have exactly what's called for, use something else. Check around the house; the Goodwill bag can be a treasure trove of old curtains or mismatched socks and shoes. And look in thrift stores. You may stumble across just what you need for practically nothing.

All of the costumes in this book use makeup instead of masks. Making up your face in a ghoulish style is an exciting way to create a unique look of your own. Another advantage of makeup is that you won't be stumbling around the sidewalk as you try to get from one house to another. You can see where you're going instead of trying to peer through tiny mask eyeholes.

Give yourself enough time to play around with the bizarre effects you can get with makeup. If you have access to theatrical greasepaints, by all means use them. But professional equipment is not necessary to achieve incredibly scary or weird looks. Depending on the costume, you will need one or more of the following items: black or dark brown eye pencil, various colors of eye shadow, red lip pencil, lipstick, flesh-colored liquid makeup. Many women have a boxful of odd items of makeup that they never use stuck in the back of a cupboard. Ask around and see if you can lay your hands on what you need. If you have to buy some, go to the dime store or discount variety store. Your makeup shouldn't cost more than a couple of dollars.

You may want to buy or borrow a small box of Cray-pas. These are nontoxic coloring sticks that are not waxy. A box of twelve colors costs less than $1.50 at stationery, art supply, and toy stores. They go on easily and make nice bright colors on your skin. The advantage of having a box of these is that you will have all the possible color combinations you could want for your face makeup.

One item you definitely will need is a small jar of inexpensive cold cream, for putting on and taking off your makeup. The idea is to apply makeup on top of a cold cream base and not directly on your skin. This way you won't be walking around school for several days with a faint bluish or sickly green tinge on your face.

When you want to remove your makeup, use cold cream and Kleenex to wipe off as much of it as you can. Then use soap and warm water to get rid of the last traces.

Anything that is meant to go on some of your face is safe to use on the rest of it. Eye shadow works fine on lips and a lip pencil is perfect for red-rimmed eyes. But some brands of cosmetics cause allergic reactions in some people. If any of the makeup you use makes your skin feel itchy or sore, take it off with cold cream and use something else. And do stick with cosmetic products that are meant for your face. Nail polish is much too harsh to use as eye shadow!

For putting together your props, you'll need common household items like cardboard (from boxes or the backs of writing pads) and scissors and staples. If you have poster paints in a few basic colors, you'll find them useful for making your props and for some of the costumes.

As you plan your Halloween outing there are a few things to keep in mind to make sure it's a success. Your costume needs to be comfortable enough to wear for several hours; anything too tight or binding will spoil the fun of the evening. Also be sure you're wearing enough clothes under your costume so that you will be warm; your teeth should be chattering with fear, not cold! Observe reasonable safety precautions. Tripping over a costume that's too long or being stuck by a straight pin that should have been a safety pin won't add much to your enjoyment. And be sure to stick reflective tape on any costume you wear. This tape is designed to reflect the glare of car headlights; as you flit back and forth across the street, you want to be sure drivers can see you.

It's twice as much fun to plan your Halloween with a friend. You can help each other make costumes and together you might come up with a new and even more horrifying twist. And do plan to go out trick-or-treating with a group. It's never a good idea to wander around alone after dark—and besides, going in a group makes it more of a party.

Before you go out, be sure to eat a good dinner or a hearty snack. Then you won't be tempted to eat any of the treats you get along the way. It's sad but true that some people's Halloween treats turn out to be dangerous tricks. So take everything home and examine it carefully in a good light before eating any of it.

In fact, many people don't give candy treats anymore. They hand out things that are not to be eaten—pennies, small inexpensive toys, colored pencils, or whatever. Treats like this are fun and also safe. You might suggest this idea to your own parents.

On the last night of October you will step out of your ordinary self and into the realm of nightmare and mischief. If the other spooks you meet are scared out of their wits, you know you are a success. Happy Halloween!

THE WALKING DEAD

On Halloween night the walking dead climb out of their coffins. Their clothes are covered with graveyard mud and their eyes stare vacantly. Held in chains, they clank drearily as they stalk the streets. They only speak the terrifying words, "Trick or treat!"

COSTUME

Old jeans or dark pants: Wear jeans that you are allowed to get really filthy. Streak them with mud and smear dirt on them to get the look of having crawled through a muddy graveyard.

Ratty old shirt: This can be a T-shirt, a sweat shirt, anything that is about to go into the ragbag. Decide whether you were done in by a bullet or a knife, and make either a round hole or a jagged slit over your heart. (Don't forget to add a bullet hole on the back of your shirt, too.) Paint or draw with black

13

around the edges of the hole or slit. Then dribble red poster paint down from the bullet hole or knife slit to look like dried blood. (If it's cold out, wear an old turtleneck or sweater under the costume shirt.)

Beat-up shoes and wrinkled socks: Any shoes and socks will do, as long as they don't look neat and clean!

MAKEUP

Gray face: For the dead look, cover your face and neck with a thin film of cold cream and then smooth on gray makeup. You can use gray eye shadow or Cray-pas, or add a drop or two of black eye liner to light-colored liquid makeup.

Black eye sockets, lips, and nostrils: Cray-pas or soft eye pencil will work best for drawing the enlarged black nostrils. Go around the edge of each nostril and extend the black upward to make the nostril look bigger. Use black on your lips; also smudge it around the whole socket of each eye.

Staring eyes: For a vacant, empty look, draw a line of white along each upper and lower eyelid near your lashes. Use white eye shadow or Cray-pas.

Scar: Decide where you want your scar: fore-

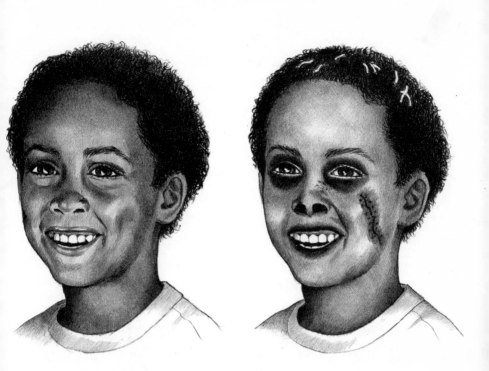

head, cheek, chin, or wherever. Make a wide, crooked line with blue and dark red Cray-pas and smudge it a little to look swollen and bruised. Then use an eye pencil to draw a narrow line of black through the middle of it for the scar line. A line of small black dots on each side of the scar will look like the holes left by stitches.

Scarred gray hands (optional): Use the same gray makeup on the backs of your hands if you want to. Add a scar to keep up the ghoulish appearance.

Worms (optional): Short pieces of cold cooked

spaghetti can be sprinkled over your hair and costume for a really repulsive look!

Chains: Use any lightweight chain you have around the house. A dog leash or stake-out chain is perfect. Or you might find some leftover chain from a swag lamp or hanging plant pot. You can always buy some chain at a hardware store: 3 or 4 feet will be enough. Get big links if you can, but make sure the chain is not too heavy to wear.

Drape the chain loosely across your body from shoulder to waist in a loop or two. Wrap the rest of the chain around your waist and let the end dangle down. Tie the chain together with string or twist ties so it won't fall off. You can add loops of chain at your wrist if you have extra.

Trick or treat bag: A scruffy cloth bag would be best, but a rumpled brown paper shopping bag will also do fine.

SAFETY TIP

With silver reflective tape, make diagonal lines across the back of your shirt in the same direction as your chains.

BLACK CAT

Black cats accompany witches on their broomsticks on Halloween night. They swoop through the air with eerie howls and they help the witches brew all kinds of mischief. Maybe this is why people think a black cat crossing their path brings bad luck.

COSTUME

Black tights or pants: Tights are really best for this costume. If it's too cold, however, you can wear black pants that are fairly tight. To keep the legs from flapping and spoiling the sleek, catlike look, wrap black yarn or cord in spirals from knee to ankle.

Black turtleneck or sweater: This, too, should be closefitting and long sleeved. The idea is to cover your whole body neatly in black. A turtleneck leotard would also work well.

Black shoes or large black socks to cover shoes: Black ballet slippers are perfect;

you'll be able to walk stealthily and gracefully. But any black shoes will do. Or you can cover your shoes with black knee socks; use old, worn-out ones or get really cheap ones, because they'll be ruined before the night is over.

Black hood with ears: You need about 1 yard of black fabric. If you don't have any at home that you can use, get whatever is cheapest; soft lining material is usually inexpensive. Cut out a rectangle 12 inches by 22 inches. Fold it as shown in the drawing

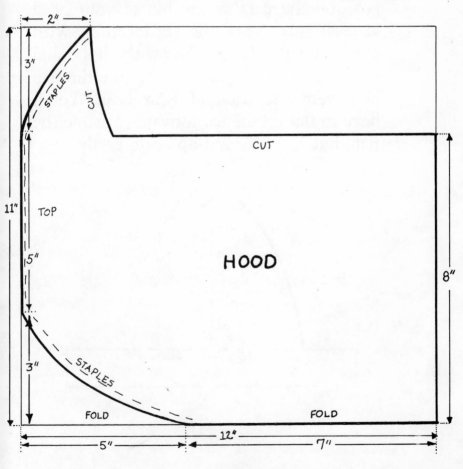

and cut off the top corners. Staple the cut corner edges and the top edge together. Make a line as in the drawing and cut along it to meet the top front edge. Turn the hood right side out so the staples won't show.

For ears, use thin cardboard; the back of a writing pad works fine. Cut out two ears as in the drawing. Fold the flap all the way back. Bend the ear gently forward over your finger to make it cupped. Paint the whole ear black on both sides with poster paint. Put on the hood. Then look in a mirror and position the ears at the top of your head at each side. Mark the ear locations with chalk or tape. Then take off the hood and staple each ear in place. Make sure the flap is toward the back of your head. You'll have to flatten the ear forward to staple the flap, but it will stand up again easily.

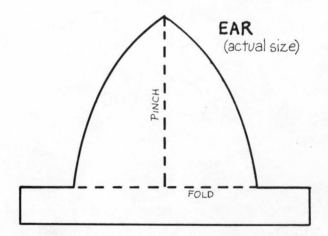

EAR
(actual size)

PINCH

FOLD

When you're ready to get into costume, use a safety pin to hold the hood closed under your chin. Tuck the bottom edge of the hood into your turtleneck.

Black tail: Use the same black fabric to make the tail. Fold over about 3 inches of the fabric along the 2-foot edge as in the drawing. Staple the material together 2 inches from the fold so you have a 2-inch-wide tube of fabric. Cut off the excess material. Staple one end of the tube closed. Then turn the tube right side out so the staples won't show; the easiest way to do this is to pull the tube over a yardstick, starting at the closed end.

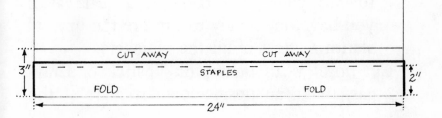

TAIL

CUT AWAY   CUT AWAY

3″   STAPLES   2″

FOLD   FOLD

24″

Roll up a sheet or two of newspaper fairly tightly and insert the roll in the fabric tube. When you're ready to go out, fold over the open end of the tail and safety-pin it to the waist of your tights or pants in the center of your back.

MAKEUP

Black whiskers: Cover your face with a thin film of cold cream. Then draw the whiskers with black eye pencil or Cray-pas. Eye whiskers slant up and outward from the outer corner of each eye, the center of your eyelid, and the space between those two. Extend them up to your eyebrow level; the outer whisker will extend to your temple.

At the inner corner of each eyebrow, draw two or three slightly curved whiskers that extend up onto your forehead, beside the point of the hood.

Cheek whiskers start a little below the outside corners of your nose. Three or four long curving lines go across each cheek toward your ears. Look at a real cat if you have one handy to capture the upward slanting effect of all the whiskers.

Cat nose: With light pink lipstick or Cray-pas, make an upside-down triangle at the

tip of your nose. Then use black eye pencil
to draw a line straight down from your nose
to your upper lip.

Pink mouth (optional): Light pink lipstick
can give the appearance of a cat's small

pink mouth. Don't extend the lipstick all the way to the corners of your mouth; cover only the wide center section of your lips.

PROPS

Trick or treat bag: Make a black cat bag to go with your costume. Cut the largest rectangle you can from the leftover black fabric; it should be about 2 feet by 2½ feet. Fold it in half crosswise and staple the sides together. Turn it right side out. Now cut two strips from the leftover fabric; make them about 12 inches long and 1 inch wide. Staple these to the top of your bag for shopping-bag-style handles. If you like, paint a design on the bag with white or silver paint or even fluorescent paint; it might be a crescent moon or a cat's face.

SAFETY TIP

Since the cat costume is all black, you'll be almost invisible as you roam the dark streets. Make stripes down your back with reflective tape so drivers will know you're there. Reflective tape can also be used for the design on your bag.

DEVIL

Of course devils are famous mischief-makers. On October 31, they are responsible for a lot of pranks and tricks. Practice leaping out unexpectedly from behind trees and scaring people with a devilish laugh.

COSTUME

Red tights or pants or long underwear: Red is the devil's color, and your costume should be as skintight as possible. So if you don't have red tights or ski underwear, use the tightest fitting pants you can find. Red yarn or cord in a spiral down your leg will hold the pants close to your skin.

Red turtleneck or sweater: Here again, the fit should be tight. A thermal underwear top will work fine, or a red leotard.

Large red socks over shoes, or boots: For the totally red look, buy a cheap pair of bright red socks in a size that will fit over whatever shoes you'll wear. Get these at the dime store or variety store, because they'll be wrecked by the time you're finished.

A she-devil might wear dark-colored boots with heels over red tights.

Red hood with horns: You need about a yard of red fabric. If you have to buy it, lining material is probably the cheapest.

Make a hood just like the Black Cat hood (see page 19). Turn it right side out. Cut out two horns from thin cardboard, such as the back of a writing pad. Paint them red on both sides, including the tab, with poster paint. Fold the tab back and, with the hood on, position the horns near the front of your head with the points facing inward. Mark the positions with chalk or tape. Then take off the hood and staple the tabs in place. When you wear the hood, fasten it under your chin with a safety pin.

Red tail: Make a red tail with the red fabric; follow the directions for the Black Cat tail on page 21. Cut a triangle about 3 inches on each side from thin cardboard and paint it red. Staple it to the end of the tail for the devilish look. When you put on your costume, fold over the open end of the tail and pin it to the back of your costume at your waist.

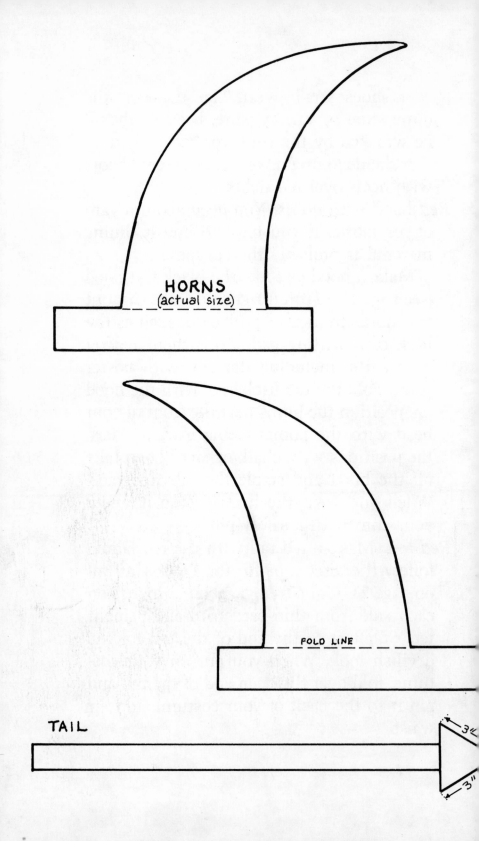

HORNS
(actual size)

FOLD LINE

TAIL

3"

3"

Red gloves (optional): If you have some, they'll add to your devilish look!

MAKEUP

Red face: Spread a thin film of cold cream over your whole face. Then cover your face with red. Red Cray-pas work best; they give a nice bright color. You can use rouge, but it won't be as colorful. White-out the outer half of each eyebrow with white eye shadow stick or Cray-pas, and then cover the white with red.

Black eyebrows and eye lines: With black or dark eye pencil, extend the slanted lines of

your eyebrows down to your nose—they should almost meet. Then draw lines from the top of each eyebrow arch upward onto your forehead.

Draw a dark line along your whole upper eyelid, and extend it upward at the outer corner. Then draw a line just under your lower eyelashes from the center of your eye to the outer corner to meet the upper line.

Black mustache: With short up-and-down strokes, draw a narrow mustache along your upper lip. At the corners, extend it down to below your lower lip. Draw the ends of the mustache in an upward curl if you want.

PROPS

Pitchfork: If you can find one, use a broom handle or straight stick for the pitchfork. Then cut the fork end out of cardboard; the back of an 8-inch by 11-inch writing pad is a good size. Bend the tab around the end of the stick and use tape or rubber bands to hold it in place. Then paint the whole thing with red paint, or fluorescent red paint if you have it.

If you can't find a stick, you can make the whole pitchfork out of cardboard and

30

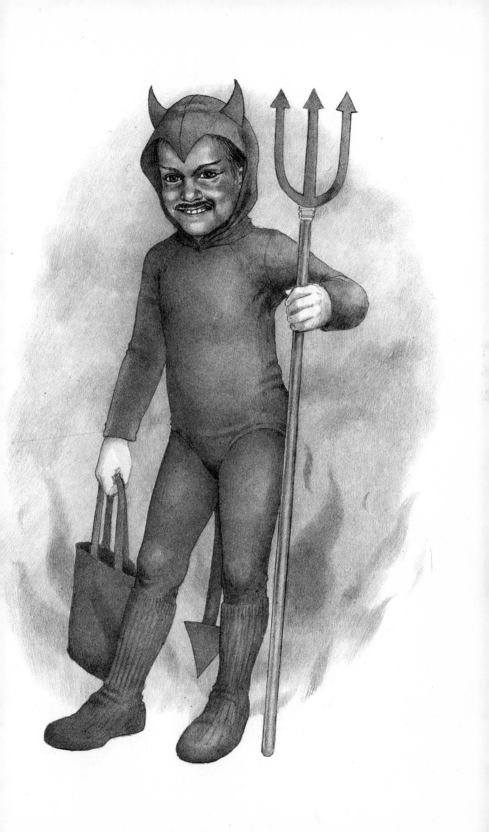

PITCHFORK
enlarge 50%

paint it. Use heavy corrugated cardboard so the pitchfork handle won't get bent or broken.

Trick or treat bag: Use the leftover red fabric to make a bag; follow the directions for the Black Cat bag on page 24. Or use a regular brown shopping bag with handles. Paint it red with a yellow flame design; if you have fluorescent paint, this will look really fiery.

SAFETY TIP

Make any design you like on the back of your costume with red reflective tape. It won't be noticeable close up, but it will shine in the glare of headlights.

DRACULA

Famous in legend and lore, Dracula is usually seen nowadays on late-night TV. Won't your neighbors be surprised to see him in person when they open their doors on Halloween night!

COSTUME

White dress shirt: If you have a plain white shirt with buttons and a collar, wear that. Of course, a fancy one with ruffles or pleats is even better. But if you can't find either, why not create that look with an old white T-shirt? Use a black marking pen to draw on a collar and buttons down the front.

Dark pants, shoes, and socks: Wear real trousers with creases down the front to help create a formal look. If you don't own any of these, at least iron your jeans!

Dark bow tie: With a regular shirt, you can use either a clip-on or real bow tie. But if you've created a dress shirt look with a T-shirt, you'll need a tie you can pin to it. Make one out of crepe paper or wide black ribbon; then safety-pin it between your phony collar points.

Opera cape: If someone you know has a long, full dark cape you can borrow, that's terrific. It may be possible to find one in a thrift shop, but it's likely to be expensive. So you may want to make one. Buy 2 yards of black lining material, the shiny, slippery kind. Lay the fabric flat. In the center of one long side, cut out a small half circle to fit around the back of your neck. Cut off the two bottom corners of the fabric as in the drawing.

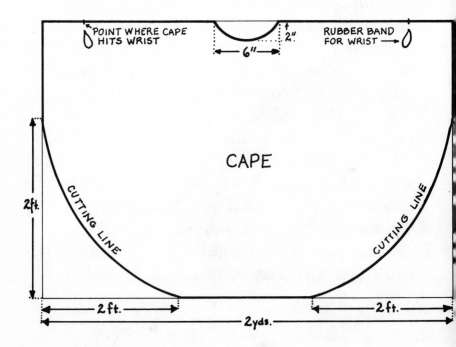

Try on the cape and mark the top edge where the cape hits your wrists. Take it off again and staple a rubber band to each side of the top edge. These will hold the cape to your wrists and allow you to sweep grandly through the evening.

When you're ready to put on your cape and go out, use tape to attach it to your shirt at the back of your neck. If your shirt has a collar, tape the cape under it. If not, attach the edge of the cape to the neckband of your T-shirt.

Long muffler (optional): If you're wearing a collarless shirt (or if it's a cold night), a trailing scarf around your neck will be a big help. It can be any long elegant-looking scarf or piece of fabric, but it will look best if it's dark in color or blood red. Knot it at one side of your neck and drape one end down your back and the other across your chest. This will hide the fact that your shirt and cape have no collars.

MAKEUP

Slicked-back hair: Comb your hair straight back away from your face. If it will stay that way with just water, that's fine. But if it's too curly and springs up, use a little hair cream or Vaseline to hold it flat and close to your head. Or try hair spray to hold it in place. If you want, make a widow's peak (see page 44).

White face: Cover your whole face, including your eyelids, with a film of cold cream. For Dracula's bloodless look, use white Craypas everywhere except on your eyelids and lips.

Dark hollows and lines: Use black or dark brown eye pencil to produce a hungry, hollow-cheeked look. Suck in your cheeks and use the side of the pencil point to make two or three lines in the hollow under each cheekbone. Smudge these with your fingers to blend the color. Do the same at each temple. Now draw slanted lines, starting at the outside edge of your nostrils, to the corners of your mouth for a fierce expression.

Vampire eyes: With the eye pencil, darken your upper eyelids and the soft area under each eye. Don't smudge this too much; it should be very dark around your eyes, fading a little toward your eyebrows. If you have a lip pencil with a sharp point, carefully draw a narrow line of red just under your lower eyelashes. You might be able to do this with a thin eyeliner brush and lipstick or creme rouge; just be sure the red line is very narrow.

Bushy eyebrows: Use a sharp eye pencil to darken and thicken your eyebrows. Don't draw across your whole eyebrow. Make short up-and-down strokes, extending your eyebrows so they almost meet over your nose and giving the outer ends a slight upward slant.

Vampire lips: For a dark, blood-red effect, use the eye pencil to blacken your lips first. Then put on dark red or plum-colored lipstick over the black.

Fangs (optional): Fangs add a lot to Dracula's gruesome look. They are widely available around Halloween, and quite inexpensive.

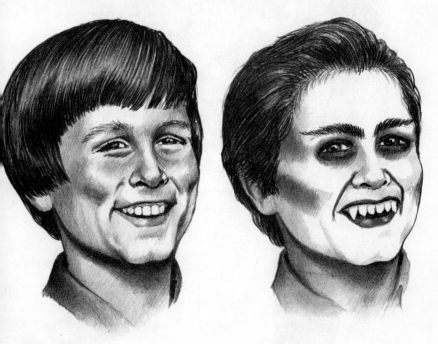

PROPS

Trick or treat bag: Dracula's bag should not be too noticeable, or it will detract from his elegant formal appearance. A drawstring bag slung over one shoulder under your cape would be best. If you use a regular paper shopping bag, try painting it black to blend in with your outfit.

SAFETY TIP

Like many figures of terror, Dracula is dressed almost entirely in black. Make a large "D" with reflective tape on the back of your cape. Or make a stripe with reflective tape down the backs of your pants legs below the cape.

VAMPIRELLA

Dressed in elegant evening clothes, Vampirella is like a deadly panther on the prowl. She's a beautiful and glamorous companion for her fellow vampire, Dracula.

COSTUME

Long skirt or pants: Since Vampirella is dressed in rather formal evening clothes, either a long skirt or dressy pants will work well. Try to find something in a dark color like black or burgundy and a rich fabric like velveteen or satin.

Blouse or top: A white ruffled blouse will be fine. Or maybe you can borrow an old sequined top or metallic knit in gold or silver. The idea is to be "dressed to kill."

Shoes and socks: Wear whatever goes with the rest of your fancy outfit—boots, high heels, ballet slippers. Just make sure you can walk in them comfortably. You can use any sort of stockings, tights, or socks since they won't show.

Cape: Ideally you want a long, flowing black velvet cape. But unless you can borrow one or find one cheap in a thrift shop, you'll need to make a cape. Follow the directions for Dracula's cape (page 34). Instead of taping it to your collar, staple some ribbon to the neckline of the cape and tie it. (If you can also tape it to your top, it will stay on your shoulders better.)

Jewelry: Look for costume jewelry that will go with your outfit. Remember that Vampirella is dressed for a fancy evening, so a fake ruby pendant or ropes of glittering pretend diamonds and sapphires are great. If you have a big, gaudy ring or two, wear them as well.

MAKEUP

Hair: Traditionally Vampirella has long dark hair parted in the center and hanging straight. But don't worry if yours is short and blond and curly. What you want to achieve is a fairly severe and sophisticated look. Comb your hair straight back from your face. Use a little hair cream or Vaseline to hold it flat and close to your head. If you need to, use a couple of bobby pins or a plain hair band to keep it away from your face so your gaunt pallor will show.

White face: Smooth a thin film of cold cream all over your face, eyelids, and mouth. Use white Cray-pas to whiten your entire face except your eyelids and lips. Also white-out the outer half of your eyebrows.

Cheek and under-eye hollows: With the side of a dark eye pencil, make a couple of strokes slanting across your cheeks under your cheekbones. Smudge them with your fingers to give you a hungry look. Do the same thing under your eyes. You don't want really black areas but grayish smudges that look sunken.

Vampirella eyes: Cover your whole upper eyelid clear up to your eyebrows with eye shadow in a pale sickly color—green, lavender, silver, frosted brown. You can apply this with a lavish hand. Then use the dark eye pencil to make upward-slanting winged eyebrows. Draw these with long strokes over the inner half of your own eyebrows and then up and out onto your forehead.

Use the eye pencil to make dark lines along your upper and lower eyelids next to the lashes. Extend the line out from the outer corner of each eye a little way, parallel to the eyebrow line.

Blood-red lips: Use the darkest red or brown lipstick you can find. If it doesn't look gruesome enough, darken your lips with the eye pencil and then apply lipstick over it.

Fangs (optional): Like Dracula, Vampirella needs fangs to puncture her victims' necks. You can buy these for very little money wherever Halloween items are sold.

Red fingernails (optional): Long, blood-red talons are one of Vampirella's trademarks. You can paint your own nails with cheap

scarlet nail polish. Or you may want to buy a set of inexpensive false nails. You can get them at a dime store and they are easy to apply. Paint them red or purple.

Widow's peak (optional): For some reason the hair of female vampires often grows in a widow's peak (a point in the center of the forehead). If you have dark hair, you can draw one or extend your own. Draw long smooth lines with the eye pencil from a point in the middle of your forehead and extending up into your own hairline.

PROPS

Trick or treat bag: Of course you can use whatever you like. But for a bag that goes well with your glamorous costume, try making a drawstring bag out of some left-over fancy fabric—black silky lining material would be great. Cut a piece that when folded in half looks like a small pillowcase. Staple the sides closed. Then turn down the top edge all the way around and staple it to hold it in place. Turn the bag right side out and run a length of ribbon or string through the hem in the top edge. Knot the ends of the string together so you can hang the bag over your wrist or shoulder.

Even if you're wearing a shiny top, drivers won't be able to see you from behind in your black cape. Make a large "V" on the back of your cape or skirt with silver reflective tape. Or use the tape to make any design you like—it will just add to your glittery look.

OGRE

"Fee, fie, fo, fum!" An ogre's dread syllables are enough to inspire shrieks of terror in everyone who hears them. Ogres come in a wide variety of shapes. This one happens to have an extra eye and a humped shoulder. But every ogre swings a large club in one hand as he stomps around in search of trick or treat goodies.

COSTUME

Old jeans: Ogres are not very well dressed, so you can wear any scruffy pants or jeans. If they have holes or frayed hems, all the better.

Mismatched shoes and socks: Wear two different kinds of socks and two different shoes as well. If you can find an old shoe that is much too large for you, stuff the front and back with newspaper so it will stay on your foot. This will give a good impression of mismatched feet!

Humped shoulder and tunic top: When you are dressing to go out, first put on a sweater or turtleneck or whatever will be warm enough. Over this you will be wearing only a shirt-tunic.

For the hump you need a small bath towel and some string or yarn. Fold the towel in quarters the long way and then in half. Drape it over one shoulder so that about one third hangs down in front and the other two thirds hangs down your back. Tie the string across the towel, over your shoulder, then under one arm and across your chest in a harness. This will keep the towel from slipping off your shoulder or down your back as you walk around.

To make the tunic, you need an old shirt that's too big for you. Ask your dad if he's got one that's ready for the ragbag—it will be pretty well ruined by the time you're done with it. Put the shirt on over your hump and belt it with rope or any old belt. Then mark places for a couple of pockets either below or above the belt. Cut out pockets from a brown paper shopping bag or scraps of fabric and staple them in place. Use a felt-tip marking pen to label your pockets. Labels like "Bats," "Live Rats," and "Snakes" have the right ogre feel. Red poster paint blood dripping down the tunic from one or more of the pockets adds a nice look of horror. And if you can round up an old rubber snake or small stuffed animal to have peeking out of the top of one pocket, so much the better.

Cap: An old woolen knit ski cap is perfect for topping off the ogre. Pull it down low over your ears and push all your hair under it. Toss a few twigs and dry leaves on top of the cap so you won't look too neat.

MAKEUP

Lumpy face: In addition to his misshapen body, the ogre has a hideous lumpy face. After applying a thin layer of cold cream all over your face, including your eyelids and lips, use Karo syrup and wisps of cotton to make lumps (see directions on page 80). You might want them on one side of your nose and on one cheek and over part of your chin. Leave your forehead free of lumps so there will be room for your third eye, and don't put them close to your mouth or they'll fall off when you talk.

Mix some flesh-tone liquid makeup with water in a saucer (you'll need about twice as much water as makeup). Using a small

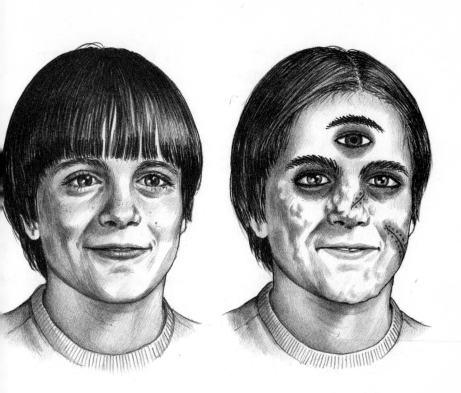

paintbrush, dab the watery makeup on the cotton until it's soaked and lumpy looking. Spread full strength makeup over the rest of your face, being careful not to dislodge your lumps.

Ogre eyes: After you have given the makeup on your face a few minutes to dry, you are ready to do your eyes. (The cotton won't dry—just be careful about bumping it with your fingers as you work.) Use dark eye pencil to draw a third eyeball, eye outline, and eyebrow in the middle of your forehead. Try to make it about the same size as your own eyes; fill in with white and brown or blue to make it look real. Now you are ready to make up all three eyes. Smudge green eye shadow on the upper and lower lids. This gives a sickly, sleepless look. Using a dark eyebrow pencil, line the upper and lower lids and darken all the eyebrows to look as much alike as possible. Then, with a lip pencil, draw a thin red line just above and below all three eyes.

Scar: Ogres have rather bashed-up faces and all of them have at least one scar. Use red and blue Cray-pas to make a wide bruised area where you want your scar. Draw the scar line with a sharp dark eyebrow pencil and make a line of dark dots on both sides of the scar for stitch marks.

PROPS

Club: If you have a Fat Bat (a short, thick, hollow plastic baseball bat) or can borrow one, it's just the right shape for a club. Unfortunately, they usually come in bright solid colors, so you need to do something to disguise this. Try covering it with a thick layer of goopy mud and letting it dry. Or if

you have some old elastic bandaging, wrap that around the bat in a spiral. And you can always papier-mâché the outside of the bat (dip strips of newspaper in a flour-and-water mixture and apply them in layers all over the bat). If you don't have a Fat Bat, make a club out of a thick roll of newspaper held together with rubber bands to form a fatter club end and a slimmer handle. Papier-mâché the whole thing and then paint it brown or gray.

Trick or treat bag: Use something fairly scruffy like a rumpled shopping bag or an old canvas knapsack. Ogres don't go in for decoration.

SAFETY TIP

Even though the ogre costume will probably be light in color, use reflective tape to form a club on the back of your tunic. It's only fair to give people a chance to run away and hide from you while they still can!

WEREWOLF

On Halloween werewolves join all the other creatures of the night. Werewolves are human beings who can transform themselves into wolves when the moon is full. The transformation is terrifying to behold, as hair (or is it fur?) grows over a person's smooth cheeks and forehead, and human speech dissolves into wolfish snarls.

COSTUME

Ordinary casual clothes: Since a werewolf can be anyone at all, even your best friend, you can wear whatever you want. Jeans and a sweat shirt are fine. But you might want to dress up in a businesslike trench coat and good pants or skirt to make the contrast with your wolfish face more horrifying.

Hair: Before you start, put a thin film of cold cream over your whole face, including your eyelids and lips. Then, if your hair is very short and straight, use a wet comb to flatten it all straight back, away from your face.

If your hair is long enough to put up, pull it straight back and pin it up at the back of your head in a smooth flat roll or twist.

If your hair is medium length, pull it straight back away from your face as far as possible. Use a hair band to hold the front part flat and let the back of your hair fall freely.

Dark wolf lines: Outline each eye with dark brown or black eye pencil. Then, starting at the inside of the bridge of your nose, use short, firm strokes to fill in the whole area at the side of your nose and under your eye halfway across. Do the same on your upper eyelid, darkening the whole eyelid halfway across and then letting the dark color merge downward into the line above your lashes.

Now squint and look in the mirror. Draw two or three lines out and up from the outer corner of each eye, following the squint lines.

For werewolf eyebrows, start in the middle of the bridge of your nose so the brows will meet. Draw short diagonal strokes along your whole eyebrow, slanting them up onto your forehead a bit. They should look bushy and fierce.

Starting at the side of the bridge of your nose, draw a long line down along the edge of your nose. Continue this line along the smile crease that forms from the corner of each nostril to the corner of your mouth. Now draw a curved line around the rounded outside of your nostril; it will meet the first line as it starts down toward your mouth.

Next, starting again at the side of the bridge of your nose, draw a diagonal line down across your cheek toward the corner of your jaw. It should be halfway between the line under your eye and the line that goes down toward your mouth.

Smudge black color on the underside of your nose in the middle and around each nostril. Fill in the indentation above the middle of your mouth with black, and darken your lips completely with the eye pencil.

Werewolf fur: To make good werewolf fur, the best thing to use is spun yarn. This kind of yarn is not twisted or plied; when you unravel it, it gets fluffy instead of forming individual thin strands. (Spun yarn is sometimes called roving wool.) You can get either acrylic or wool yarn; all Icelandic yarn is spun. You don't need much; 2 yards is plenty. So if you know someone who just made a sweater from brown Icelandic wool yarn, see if there's a couple of yards left over. Otherwise buy the cheapest you can find; be sure to get a color that will blend with your own hair color.

Cut ten or twelve 6- to 8-inch pieces of the yarn and pull them apart so you have longish pieces of fluff. Keep these dry on a plate or a sheet of paper.

With your fingers, spread Karo syrup from your cheekbone to your ear, down to the corner of your jaw, and along your jawline almost to the point of your chin. Fill in the area of your cheek between these lines with the syrup. Then spread Karo syrup from the point where your eyebrows meet upward in a thin triangle to your hairline. Finally, spread the syrup from the highest point of each eyebrow up in a diagonal line to your hairline.

Rinse your hands and dry them before handling the yarn (you'll have to keep rinsing off the syrup as you go or the yarn will get matted and stuck together). Take the fluffy pieces of yarn one at a time and lay them on your face over the syrup. Start at the top of your face; the yarn goes from the bridge of your nose across the syrup and merges with your own hair. Lay the pieces in place gently; they will stick easily.

When you finish the first section, do your eyebrows. Only a few strands are needed on each side; lay them across the syrup path and let the upper ends merge into your hair. Now do your cheeks. Again, start each piece just past the patch of syrup and let the other end blend into your hair. The fur should lie in an upward slanting direction all across your cheek, and a few pieces should creep down toward the point of your chin.

Keep adding more yarn wisps until they don't stick any more to the syrup. Pat the fur gently in place; if your fingers feel sticky spots, add a few more wisps. This sounds a lot more tedious than it is; the process goes very fast and the results are spectacular!

If you like, it's a nice touch to add werewolf fur to the backs of your hands. Spread a line of syrup along each finger tendon as far as the first knuckle. Then add wisps of yarn along each line. You don't need very much to get the furry effect.

Fangs (optional): Buy an inexpensive set of lower fangs to complete your fearsome look. Be sure to push your lower jaw forward so you'll look really threatening as you trick or treat.

PROPS

Trick or treat bag: Choose a bag that is in keeping with the kind of outfit your werewolf is wearing on its human body. A business person might carry an old briefcase; a well-dressed shopper could have a shopping bag from a fancy store. A jogger would of

course have an athletic equipment bag. Use your imagination; the contrast between your human attire and your werewolf face and hands is part of the fun.

SAFETY TIP

No matter what you wear, you don't want to be invisible. Add a few stripes of reflective tape to the back of your costume to let people know the werewolf is on the prowl.

PIRATE

Here's your chance to lead a gang of pirates. Walk with a swagger and look as ferocious as you can. Sing a sea chantey or two to let people know you're coming.

COSTUME

Jeans or dark pants: In the days of the pirates, knee pants were the look. So roll yours up to just below your knee.

Tights or knee socks: To cover the lower part of your legs you'll need dark tights or knee socks.

Boots or shoes: You can use whatever you have, but a dark color is best. Heavy boots or dark shoes with buckles will carry out the seagoing look. Or tie homemade buckles on your sneakers. Cut them out of gold-colored cardboard if you can find it—boxes of cards or from department stores are good sources.

Large blousy shirt: Any long sleeved, loose, and brightly colored shirt will do. The idea is that the sleeves will billow out of the armholes of the vest.

Sash or belt: A brightly colored scarf or strip of fabric, or even a gaudy necktie, will work well for a sash. It needs to be long enough to tie around your waist. Don't worry if it seems to clash with the color of your shirt—pirates like wild color combinations. If you have a belt with a big metal buckle, it will do fine instead.

Eye patch: Use thin cardboard, such as the back of a writing tablet, to make your eye patch. Draw a shape like the one shown and cut it out. You'll also need about 2½ feet of string—regular kitchen cord or anything you have around will be fine. Staple

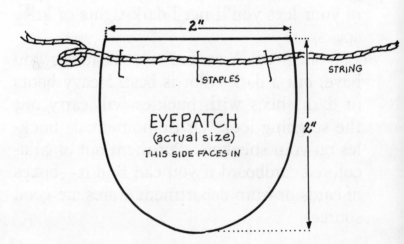

2"

STAPLES

STRING

EYEPATCH
(actual size)
THIS SIDE FACES IN

2"

the string across the top of the eye patch. Paint the patch black. You can also paint the string if you like. Put the patch over one eye and tie the string firmly at the back of your head to hold it in place. Be sure to wear the eye patch with the sharp ends of the staples facing out.

Bandana: A regular old red or blue bandana is all you need for this. Or you can use any colored scarf or even a square of fabric. Fold it diagonally in half to form a triangle. Lay it on top of your head so that the fold is across your forehead and the bandana covers the top of your head. Then tie it in back. Your bandana is very useful for keeping the sweat out of your eyes while you're heaving on the oars or in the middle of a sword fight.

Vest: If you have a vest you can wear, that's great. And it doesn't matter at all what color it is. But if you don't, it's easy to make one out of any fabric that's around. You'll need a piece of material 1½ by 2½ feet. Use a ruler and pencil, ballpoint, or chalk (whatever will show) to mark your fabric according to the diagram. Cut out the vest along the lines you drew. Match up the front and back shoulders and staple them together. Try on the vest over the shirt you plan to wear and

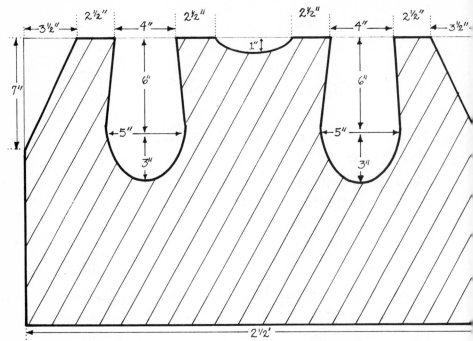

VEST

make any adjustments needed—if it's too long, trim off the bottom.

One gold earring: Pirates often wear some of their stolen spoils. If you can borrow a clip-on gold-colored hoop earring from your mom, that's great. But you can probably find a cheap pair at the dime store. Or how about using a gold-colored curtain ring? Tie a piece of thread through it to make a loop. Then loop the thread over your ear to dangle the ring just below your earlobe. If clip-on earrings pinch your ears too much, this is a perfect solution.

Heavy eyebrows: Spread a thin film of cold cream over your face. Use a black or dark brown pencil to make your eyebrows look thick and bushy. Try lots of short upward strokes to achieve this effect.

Mustache: The same eyebrow pencil will make a terrific mustache. Use long sideways strokes above your upper lip. Then continue the mustache onto your cheeks with dashing curlicue ends.

Scar: A scarred face is the reward of the pirate's violent life. A good place for your scar would be just below your eye patch. Put on

the eye patch and mark how far down on your cheekbone it comes. Use blue and red or green Cray-pas to create a disgusting swollen path for your scar. Then draw the jagged scar line and stitch marks with eyebrow pencil. (See page 15.) No one will want to look at the rest of your eye under its patch!

Skull and crossbones tattoo: Draw a skull and crossbones on the back of your hand with a sharpened eyebrow pencil or lip pencil. Then when you reach out to take your treats, everyone will know you mean business!

PROPS

Cardboard dagger: Every pirate has a dagger stuck in his sash in case of emergency. Make yours out of corrugated cardboard and big enough so everyone will see it. If you want the handle to have a rounder look you can wrap it with masking tape to pad it. Paint the handle black and the blade silver.

Cardboard hook: If you like the idea of being a one-handed pirate for one night, make a hook out of thin cardboard. It should be about the size of your cupped hand, but

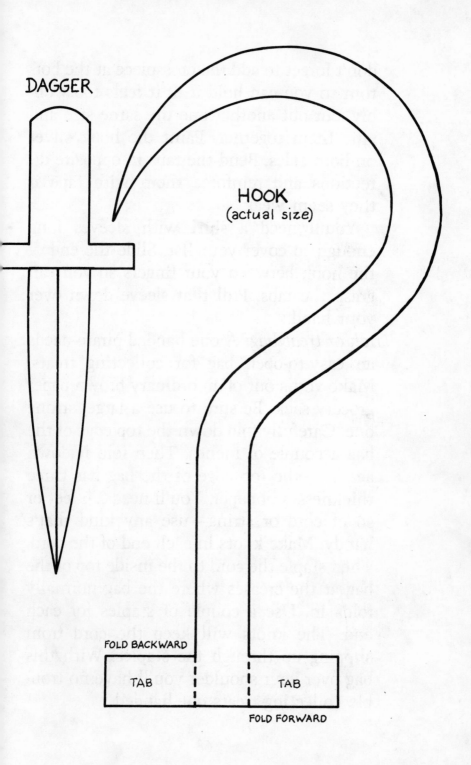

DAGGER

HOOK
(actual size)

FOLD BACKWARD

TAB

TAB

FOLD FORWARD

don't forget to add the crosspiece at the bottom so you can hold it. If it feels too wobbly, cut out another one the same size and glue them together. Paint the hook silver on both sides. Bend the tabs in opposite directions and reinforce them with tape if they seem weak.

You'll need a shirt with sleeves long enough to cover your fist. Slide the end of the hook between your fingers so you can grasp the tabs. Pull that sleeve down over your hand.

Trick or treat bag: A one-handed pirate needs an easy-to-open bag for collecting treats. Make yours out of an ordinary brown paper grocery sack. Be sure to use a large, strong one. Carefully fold down the top edge of the bag a couple of inches. Then fold it down again so the top edge of the bag has three thicknesses of paper. You'll need 2½ feet or so of cord or string—use any kind that's handy. Make knots in each end of the cord. Then staple the cord to the inside top of the bag at the creases where the bag normally folds in. Use a couple of staples for each end. The knots will keep the cord from slipping up through the staples. With this bag over your shoulder you'll have no trouble collecting treats one-handed.

Even though the pirate costume is colorful, you'll need some reflective tape on the back of the vest so motorists can see you swaggering down the street. Silver reflective tape in a skull and crossbones design will let them know you're out looking for treasure.

MUMMY

The mummy's tomb has been broken open. His eternal rest has been shattered. Now he stalks the streets in his tattered burial wrappings, doomed to carry out the mummy's curse: "Woe to anyone who opens my casket, in the name of Amon Ra!"

COSTUME

Body suit: Since your mummy wrapping will be very lightweight, you'll need something under it that will keep you warm. But you want something that is closefitting and that won't show through the wrappings too much. White or off-white clothes will be best. You might wear a long sleeved white turtleneck and tights; if it's cold, you could add another layer of white ski (thermal) underwear.

Shoes and socks: You can really wear whatever you want on your feet, but if you have a pair of lightweight slippers or ballet slippers, they will work best. Pull a pair of old white athletic socks (or a new cheap pair that are too big) over your shoes. Then you can bring the mummy wrapping down to your ankles and it will look as if it continues over your feet.

Mummy wrapping: You need a large (60 yards) roll of 1½-inch wide masking tape for your body wrapping; you need also a 5-yard roll of 3-inch-wide gauze bandaging (found in any drugstore) to wrap your head. If the gauze looks too white to match the masking tape, dip it in weak tea the day before and hang it out to dry.

Putting on your mummy wrappings will be much easier if you can get someone to help you.

Start with your ankles and work up. Wrap the tape in spirals around your leg, overlapping it slightly to cover your leg completely. Stop when you get to your knee; break off the tape. Then begin again just above where you stopped. This will allow your knee to bend as you walk.

Stop when you get to the top of your thigh and break off the tape. When both legs are done, move on to your body. Start the next section of tape in the middle of your stomach and run it down between your legs. Crisscross the tape diagonally over your hips and between your legs in a diaper look to cover as much of your bottom as you can. Then break off the tape.

Now you're ready for more spirals. Start just below your hipbones and wrap the tape around your body until you get to your underarms.

Start another piece of tape, crisscrossing over your shoulders to cover your upper chest and back. When this is finished, you're ready to do your head.

The idea is to cover as much of your head as you can, but to leave your eyes and mouth free. It may take a couple of tries before you get it covered fairly evenly. Start by taping down the end of the gauze strip under your collarbone; bring it up around your neck and over your head. Keep wrapping, and don't forget to go under your chin and across your forehead, nose, and chin. However, be careful not to wrap it too tightly around your neck; if it does feel tight, pull it gently with one finger to stretch it a little. Tape down the end when you're finished.

When your head is done, do your makeup while your arms are still moving freely.

Then go back and wrap your arms with masking tape. Start at the shoulder and move down. Stop just above the elbow; then start again below your elbow so you'll be able to move your arms. End the wrappings on your hands where your fingers begin.

When you're all finished, you may feel you look too neat and clean to be an ancient mummy. You can add tatters and dirt to look more gruesome. Strips of old sheets, cheesecloth, or stretched gauze bandaging can be wrapped over the masking tape here and there; the more raveled they are, the better.

MAKEUP

Hollow eye sockets: With a soft black or dark brown eye pencil, circle each eye. Darken

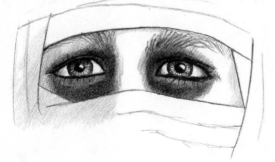

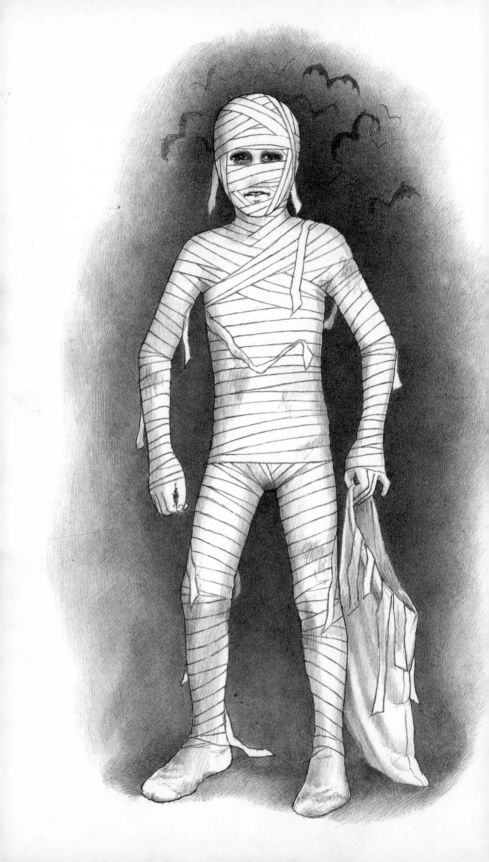

the whole upper eyelid, the hollow under the eye, and the inside of the bridge of your nose. You may have to pull the gauze away slightly to get at your eyes; smudge the color with your fingers to give yourself a skull-like look.

White face and mouth: Use white Cray-pas or eye shadow stick to whiten any part of your face that shows through the wrapping. Don't forget to cover the bridge of your nose and your lips.

PROPS

Trick or treat bag: Use an old white pillow-case to blend in with your costume. Tape or staple some raggedy pieces of gauze to the open end so they hang down; the bag will look like something you brought out of the tomb.

SAFETY TIP

The mummy costume is quite visible, since it's all white. Still, it's a good idea to wear some reflective tape. Ask your friend to make a coffin shape on your back or to write a message in some mysterious, ancient language.

WITCH

Witches usually fly through the air on broomsticks. But on Halloween you may see them walking through the streets. You can recognize a witch, even without her broomstick, by her cackling laugh.

COSTUME

Black or dark skirt: Witches are far from fashion plates, so your skirt should be a little too big for you. A longish gathered skirt with the hem half out is perfect.

Shapeless black or dark top: This can be an old sweater, shirt, cardigan, or whatever will look baggy and out of style. Make sure it's warm enough or wear more than one layer of this look.

Black or dark shoes and tights or knee socks: Again, don't wear brand-new shoes in the latest style. Witches wear old-fashioned lace-up shoes; maybe you can find a scuffed pair in a thrift shop.

Short black cape: Use one square yard of black fabric for the cape. If you have to buy it, lining material is likely to be the least expensive.

Lay the fabric flat and fold over one corner as in the drawing. The folded edge will go around your neck. When you're ready to put on the cape, pick it up carefully by the corners of the fold and drape it loosely across your shoulders. This cape is not designed to close in the front. Use safety pins to fasten the sides to your shirt; attach the cape near your shoulders, just under your

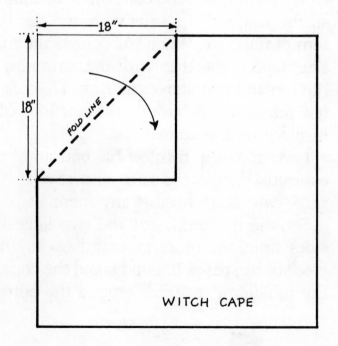

WITCH CAPE

collarbone. Gently pull up the fold at the back of your neck to look like a stand-up collar.

Witch's hat: You need a couple of large, clean brown-paper grocery bags to make the hat. Cut a rectangle 18 inches by 12 inches from a flat side of one bag. Then cut a 1-inch strip that is 2 feet long; use one narrow side and the bottom of the bag for this.

Wrap the strip of paper around your head and tape it together so that you have a ring the size your hat should be.

Make a cone from the rectangle of brown paper and hold it together at the bottom. Drop the paper ring you made over the cone. Then make the cone fatter or thinner so the ring will fit snugly around the bottom of the cone. When the cone is the right size, tape it together with masking tape at the top and just above the ring. Then use a few pieces of tape around the ring to hold it in place on the cone.

Now carefully trim off the bottom of the cone just below the ring, and remove the ring—you don't need it any more.

For the hat brim, cut the two large flat sides from the other grocery bag. Lay one piece of bag paper flat and stand the cone in the middle of it. Trace around the bottom

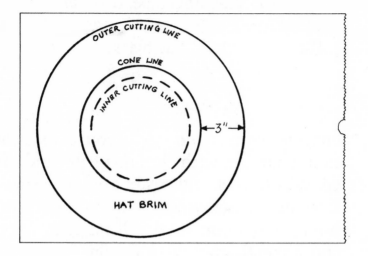

edge of the cone. Set the cone aside and draw another circle 3 inches outside the first one. Cut around the outer circle. Then carefully cut out the center of the doughnut shape, cutting a little bit *inside* the inner circle you drew.

Trace the doughnut shape on the other piece of bag paper and cut it out. Glue these two pieces together to make a stiff brim for the hat. (You can make the hat brim instead out of one piece of cardboard that is at least 12 inches square, but remember that heavy cardboard is hard to cut neatly.)

Put the cone on your head and drop the brim over it. If the hole in the brim is too small, enlarge it carefully. Tape the brim in place with masking tape to hold the hat together.

Paint the whole hat black.

MAKEUP

Lumpy nose and chin: Hold your hair away from your face with clips or a hair band and spread a film of cold cream over your whole face and under your chin. To create the lumpy look, you need a little Karo syrup and a small amount of cotton. With your fingers, spread some Karo syrup over your nose and on your chin. Rinse the syrup off your fingers before the next step!

Pull out small wisps of the cotton (you don't need much—one ball of cotton is more than enough for both nose and chin) and stick them on where you've spread the syrup. Don't be upset that it looks like a moth-eaten Santa Claus beard at this point; just be sure you stick the cotton wisps over all the syrup on your face.

Green face: Pour a little liquid makeup into a saucer. Add one drop each of green and yellow food coloring and mix with a paint-brush (like the kind that comes in water-color sets). You should have a muddy, yucky green color; if it doesn't look right, add more color or makeup until it's the shade you want. Now add a few drops of water and mix again. The makeup has to be fairly wet.

With the paintbrush, dab the green makeup all over the cotton on your nose and chin. As the cotton gets wet, it will start lumping against your skin. Gently push it with the brush to lump it up the way you want.

When you've finished your nose and chin, apply the green makeup to the rest of your face. You can do this with a cotton ball dipped in the makeup, but be careful not to disturb the lumps that are still wet. (Before you put this gunk on your skin, make sure you've got cold cream everywhere. Otherwise you may have a greenish face for a few days!) If the color on your skin doesn't match the cotton lumps, mix a new batch of makeup and don't add water to it. Then apply this to your face.

If your lumps start to come off, you may need more Karo syrup to glue them around the edges. Or you may have made them too large—too much cotton will get too heavy when it's wet.

Heavy eyebrows, hollow cheeks, and black lips: Use a dark brown or black eye pencil

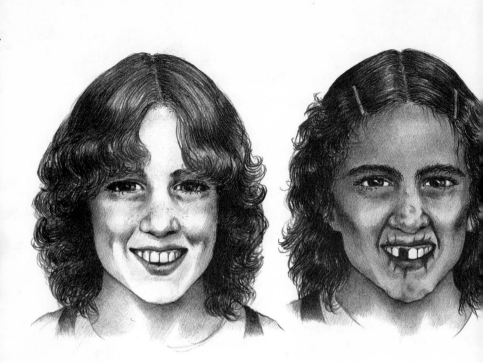

for the rest of your witch makeup. Draw thick dark eyebrows over your own eyebrows and a little below them for a scowling appearance. Extend them a bit toward your nose—this makes you look mean and angry.

Suck in your cheeks and with the side of the pencil point, draw a few strokes of black in the hollows. Smudge the color gently with your finger to make your cheeks look sunken. Then draw short wrinkle lines around your mouth.

Use the pencil like a lipstick to blacken your lips. As the color smudges, your lips will look gray and horrible.

Stringy hair (optional): Pour a spoonful of cooking oil or baby oil onto a good-sized piece of waxed paper. Now lay your comb in the oil so the teeth are coated, and pull it through your hair. (Don't worry! A thorough shampooing will get it all out afterward.)

Blackened tooth (optional): When witches cackle, their teeth are revealed. You can make yours more witchlike with a small square of black tape. Dry your tooth with a Kleenex and stick the tape on it.

PROPS

Broom (optional): Any broom will do for a witch—the rattier the better. But keep in mind that you may find it heavy to carry around if you plan a long night of trick-or-treating.

Trick or treat bag: See if you can scrounge up an old black carrier bag or a mesh shopping bag. These were once part of every household's equipment and they'd be perfect for a witch. Otherwise use a regular brown-paper shopping bag; paint it or decorate it with a black cat.

SAFETY TIP

Since a witch is dressed all in black, she's not easily visible on a dark night. Use silver reflective tape to make a crescent moon design on your hat and cape, and perhaps on your bag as well.

UNKNOWN TERROR

What is the Unknown Terror? Nobody knows! It comes from outer space and it's never before been seen by earthlings. Its blue face and white staring eyes make mere humans cower in fear. And when it says "Trick or treat!" in robotlike tones, everyone knows it's a visitor from alien galaxies.

COSTUME

Robe: The basic costume you'll make is a long robe and a matching hood. Be sure to wear warm enough clothes under the robe so you won't freeze; you can wear whatever you like since your clothes won't show.

The robe can be made out of any large piece of fabric. An old sheet is good; so is an old curtain or even a tablecloth. Any kind of fabric will do, from an oilcloth tablecloth to a velvet drape or an ordinary sheet.

Ideally the piece of fabric should be as long as twice the distance from your shoulders to your ankles; it should be as wide as the distance between your outstretched wrists. This will usually work out to be a rectangle twice as long as it is wide. But if it's a little too small in either direction, don't worry. You can improvise a perfectly good robe from any large piece or from two

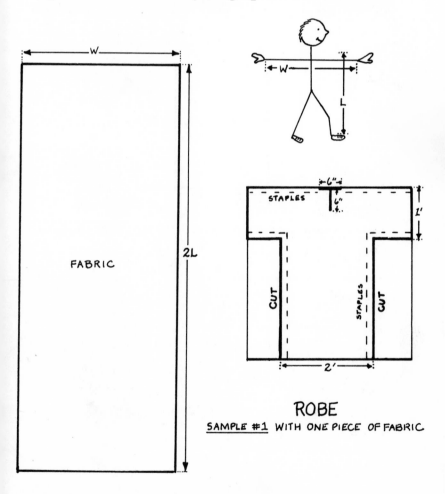

ROBE
SAMPLE #1 WITH ONE PIECE OF FABRIC

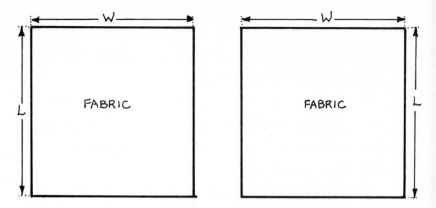

SAMPLE **2** WITH TWO PIECES OF FABRIC

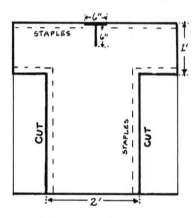

SAMPLE **3** WITH ONE PIECE OF FABRIC (TOO WIDE & NOT LONG ENOUGH)

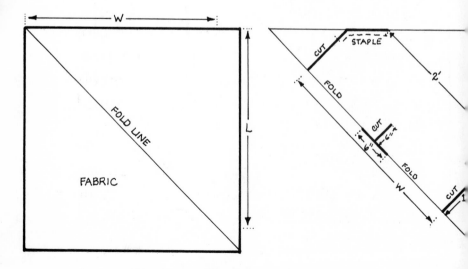

smaller pieces stapled together. Look at the drawings for some ideas.

Draw the outline of your robe on the fabric and cut it out. Staple it together as in the drawings. Don't forget to make a T-shaped slit for your head.

Remember, the Unknown Terror doesn't buy its outfits on this planet. Decorate the robe with weird signs and symbols. Use paint or reflective tape, or glue on cutouts from aluminum foil or colored cellophane. Old tinsel garlands from a Christmas tree can be stapled to the robe in strange patterns.

Shoes and socks: You can wear whatever you want on your feet—the weirder, the better. Clear plastic beach shoes or silver colored vinyl boots might strike the right note. Or decorate regular rubber boots with reflective tape. However, if your robe is short enough so your legs will show, disguise them! Old white tights can be painted with poster paints in strange designs. If you live in a warm climate, paint strange symbols directly on your bare legs. Gaudily striped knee socks would also look good.

Hood: Make a close-fitting hood like the one for the Black Cat (see page 19). You can use the same fabric you used for the robe, or something that contrasts wildly with it.

When you get dressed to go out, fasten the hood together under your chin with a safety pin. Use another pin or some tape to hold the front opening of your robe closed.

Neckpiece: Stuff a knee sock with crumpled newspaper. When you put it around your neck, push the toe into the top of the sock and safety-pin the neckpiece together.

Alien hands: Cut two triangular hands from thin cardboard (see diagram). Staple the wristband together so you can slide it on and off. Paint the hands blue to match your face, or cover them with aluminum foil. These will disguise your human hands but leave your fingers free underneath to pick up treats.

Headdress: The basic part of the headdress is a length of aluminum foil that fits around your head about where you would wear a hat. Roll up the aluminum foil piece and crimp the ends together. Cut another foil roll to arch over your head from front to

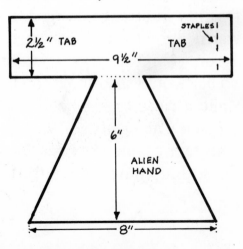

back or from side to side; attach it to the base by crimping the ends around the aluminum foil ring. You can make the arch as high as you like.

Attach long pipe cleaners around the base of the headdress for antennas and stick a Styrofoam packing bit on the end of each one. If you have one, an inexpensive tiny flashlight attached to your headdress arch will keep you in contact with your spacecraft. Or you can add another aluminum foil arch and weave colored yarn around and between the arches.

MAKEUP

Your Unknown Terror makeup is the final touch that makes you look completely inhuman.

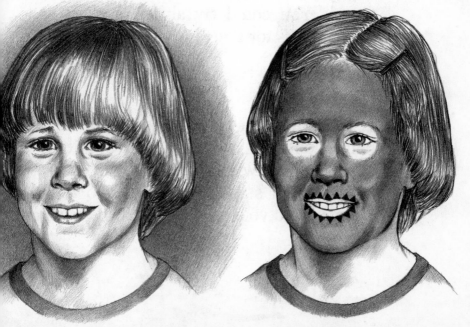

Blue face: Cover your face with a thin film of cold cream. Then use blue Cray-pas to make your skin completely blue except around your eyes. Lots of color gives an electrifying effect.

White eyes: Use white stick or creme eye shadow to cover your upper eyelids up to your eyebrows and the hollows below your eyes. Try to make a good-sized circle of white around each eye so you'll have the right kind of staring look. You can use white Cray-pas instead, but eye shadow looks more dead white.

White mouth with points: Coat your lips with white eye shadow. Using either dark eye pencil or bright red lip pencil, make small triangles at the edge of your lips pointing outward. Make the center and corner triangles first and then add one or two in between. You could try alternating red and black points for a really weird look.

PROPS

Evil eye: Draw an eye outline 6 to 8 inches across on thin cardboard and cut it out. Paint it silver with a blue eyeball. Then attach it with staples to a string so it will hang around your neck at about the level of

your navel. Use string the color of your robe so it won't be visible, or use transparent fishing line. Or paint one on your robe instead.

U.T.'s companion: A headless doll is the perfect sidekick. Sit it on your shoulder and hold it in place with masking tape. A strip of tape across its lap attaches it to your robe, and another strip around its waist holds it close to your neckpiece. If you can't find a headless doll, a good substitute is a teddy bear or other stuffed animal covered with aluminum foil.

Trick or treat bag: Paint a regular paper shopping bag silver, or cover it with aluminum foil taped to the top edge. This will rattle strangely as you carry it. Or attach streamers of foil to the top edge of the shopping bag.

SAFETY TIP

Another large evil eye on the back of your robe between your shoulders will stare down Halloween drivers. Make the outline with silver reflective tape. Then the eyeball can be a solid circle of reflective tape or a construction paper circle with a reflective tape pupil. Everyone will know that the Unknown Terror sees all!

INDEX